Gravity

MATT MULLINS

Children's Press®
An Imprint of Scholastic Inc.
New York Toronto London Auckland Sydney
Mexico City New Delhi Hong Kong
Danbury, Connecticut

Content Consultant
Suzanne E. Willis, PhD
Professor and Assistant Chair, Department of Physics
Northern Illinois University
DeKalb, Illinois

Library of Congress Cataloging-in-Publication Data

Mullins, Matt.
 Gravity / Matt Mullins.
    p. cm.—(A true book)
 Includes bibliographical references and index.
 ISBN 978-0-531-26322-8 (library binding)   ISBN 978-0-531-26584-0 (pbk.)
  1. Gravitation—Juvenile literature. 2. Gravity—Juvenile literature.
 I. Title. II. Series.
 QC178.M85 2012
 531'.14—dc22   2011009489

All rights reserved. Published in 2012 by Children's Press, an imprint of Scholastic Inc.
Printed in China 62
SCHOLASTIC, CHILDREN'S PRESS, A TRUE BOOK, and associated logos are trademarks and/or registered trademarks of Scholastic Inc.
3 4 5 6 7 8 9 10 R 21 20 19 18 17 16 15 14 13

Find the Truth!

Everything you are about to read is true *except* for one of the sentences on this page.

Which one is **TRUE**?

T or F   Gravity is a magnetic force.

T or F   Large objects bend space.

Find the answers in this book.

Claudius Ptolemy,
scientist and author

Contents

1 What Gravity Is and What It Affects

What are the differences between mass, matter, and weight?.........................7

2 How We Used to Think About Gravity

How did Galileo Galilei change people's ideas about the universe?.....................13

3 Gravity Becomes Clearer

What question did Newton ask about gravity's effect on the solar system?...................23

THE **BIG** TRUTH!

Weightlessness Hurts!

What are the side effects of being in space?.....................28

Galileo's telescope

Astronomers believe that black holes are located at the center of galaxies.

4 Einstein Explains That Space Bends

How can we show that big objects attract smaller ones? **31**

5 Gravity, Light, and Stars

What does gravity have to do with black holes? **35**

True Statistics. **43**

Resources **44**

Important Words. **46**

Index **47**

About the Author. **48**

Weightlessness in outer space

CHAPTER 1

What Gravity Is and What It Affects

You have probably seen movies or television shows about space travel. When space travelers go outside their ships, they use jet packs or tie themselves to their ships. They do this because outside their spaceships there is no force that keeps them attached to the craft. Without something to keep them attached, they would just drift off into space.

 Entering space to work outside a space shuttle or station is called spacewalking.

Gravity makes a ball roll down an incline toward the ground.

The Force of Gravity

Gravity is a mysterious attraction between objects. Gravity explains why and how fast things fall to the ground. It also explains how planets **orbit** stars and how the moon orbits Earth. Without gravity, we would not be attracted to the earth. We would fly off into space, just like space travelers outside their spaceships.

Gravity doesn't just make things fall, it also helps guide plant roots down into the soil.

Matter, mass, weight, and even gravity play roles in a game of marbles.

You can't see it, but two marbles have gravity that tugs them together.

Before we can really look at gravity, we need to understand the difference between **matter**, **mass**, and **weight**. Matter is the stuff all around you. Anything made of atoms or **molecules** is matter. All matter has mass. Mass is the amount of matter in an object.

When you weigh yourself, you are measuring the force of gravity on your body.

The mass of an object determines how much gravity it produces.

Weight is the force that a gravitational body puts on mass. That is, your weight is how much the earth pulls on your mass.

Matter is stuff. Mass is the amount of stuff. Weight is how much the earth's gravity pulls on stuff.

Keeping Things in Motion

Gravity keeps Earth and other planets moving around the sun. Gravity also makes a ball drop to the ground. When we jump up, gravity brings us back down. Gravity works on all bodies with mass, from the sun to people to the smallest cookie crumb. It works far away, and it works here on Earth.

Gravity is what makes jump rope games like this one possible.

Aristotle opened a school known as the Lyceum in Athens, Greece, in 335 B.C.E.

CHAPTER 2

How We Used to Think About Gravity

For almost 2,000 years, most people thought of gravity the same way that the Greek philosopher Aristotle explained it. Aristotle believed that objects were drawn to other objects of the same material. When you drop a rock, it falls to the ground because it has so much earth in it. He also thought heavy objects fell faster than light ones. His proof? Rocks fall faster than feathers.

Aristotle often walked when he taught. His students became known as Peripatetics, or "those who walk around."

Aristotle believed that Earth was the center of the **universe**. He thought that the sun, the planets, and stars revolved around Earth. Claudius Ptolemy, a Roman citizen living in Egypt in the second century c.e., agreed with Aristotle. Ptolemy created a model of the universe, with Earth at the center.

Ptolemy was a mathematician and geographer.

14

Ptolemy's Model

Before we knew that gravity kept Earth circling the sun, people accepted Ptolemy's model. Ptolemy believed Earth, the sun, and the planets were all attached to spheres, like giant clear balls. Earth's sphere was at the center of the universe. Moving outward from Earth, the moon's sphere was next. Then came two planets, the sun, three more planets, and finally all the stars, which were supposedly fixed on a single sphere.

Is Earth the Center?

In the 1500s, scientists began to take a different view of the universe. **Astronomers**—scientists who study the sun, planets, and stars—began to question if Earth was the center of the universe. They mapped stars and planets, and carefully recorded their movements. Observation and mathematics showed that the sun could not be circling Earth.

The word *planet* comes from Greek words meaning, "wandering star."

In 1543, Polish priest Nicolaus Copernicus wrote that a simpler explanation of planetary movement required the sun to be at the center of the universe. The Danish astronomer Tycho Brahe did not believe Copernicus, but he recorded planetary movement carefully. Before he died, Brahe gave his **data**

Tycho Brahe's inventions allowed him to make the most accurate observations possible of the stars and planets in the 1500s.

to Johannes Kepler, a German mathematician and astronomer.

Kepler replaced Brahe as the royal mathematician for Holy Roman Emperor Rudolf II.

Kepler was once Brahe's assistant. He supported Copernicus's model and continued to add to Brahe's data. Kepler realized that planets did not move in perfect circles around the sun. He proposed that planets moved in an oval pattern, called an **ellipse**. Kepler's work combined math and astronomy to accurately describe the paths that planets follow through space.

Galileo Galilei

In the 17th century, Italian astronomer Galileo Galilei contributed many important ideas to our knowledge of gravity. Galileo made fine **telescopes**. With his telescope, he observed how planets moved. When he observed that Venus had phases just as the moon does, Galileo knew that Copernicus was right. Galileo studied gravity. But like other scientists, he did not know that gravity caused planets to move the way they do.

Galileo made substantial improvements to the telescope by grinding his own lenses and increasing the power of his telescopes.

The Catholic Church had warned Galileo to stop insisting as fact that the sun was the center of the universe. Galileo argued his views in his influential book, *Dialogue Concerning the Two Chief World Systems*. It was published in 1632. This angered the Church, and the Pope had Galileo arrested.

Dialogue became an instant best seller.

Traditionally, scientific books were written in Latin. Galileo's *Dialogue* was written in Italian, so anyone could read it.

Representatives of the Church ran Galileo's trial in 1633.

After a trial in 1633, Galileo was put under house arrest. He spent the rest of his life, nine years, at his home in Florence, Italy. There Galileo worked on the motion of falling things. He wrote that falling objects increase in speed as they fall. He also claimed that no matter what they weigh, objects fall at the same, increasing speed. Galileo proved his belief with scientific experiments.

CHAPTER 3

Gravity Becomes Clearer

Sir Isaac Newton was an English mathematician, philosopher, and astronomer. He lived from 1642 to 1727. An old story claims that he was sitting under an apple tree when an apple fell and struck his head. Newton wondered if the force that had caused the apple to fall reached as far as the moon. This question changed the way scientists thought about gravity.

Newton himself told friends that watching an apple fall had inspired him.

The moon's gravity is strong enough to help create the ocean tides on Earth.

Earth's gravity pulls on the moon, and the moon's gravity pulls on Earth.

To Newton, the question was not whether gravity existed, but whether it extended great distances from Earth. We know from his writings that Newton was already thinking that gravity could extend to the moon even before he was "hit" on the head with the apple. If this were true, he thought, could gravity be the force that held the moon in its orbit around Earth?

Creating a Theory

The moon speeds through space. If gravity from Earth attracts it, Newton thought, it would move around Earth rather than fly off into space. Newton took the idea of gravity affecting small things on Earth and applied it to things outside Earth. He pulled his ideas about gravity together into one theory.

There is an old tale that Newton dropped a large and a small object from a tower at the same time to prove that all objects fall at the same speed, no matter what they weigh.

Newton's Laws

In 1686, Newton published *Principia*, a three-part work that describes his laws of gravity and motion, and the motion of planets. These laws explained why Kepler's theories on the ways planets move were correct. The laws also proved Galileo's work on falling objects. Newton's work made sense of the way the sun and planets are arranged. He even explained that high and low tides are caused by gravity from the sun and the moon.

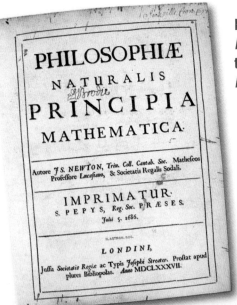

Newton's Latin title *Philosophiae Naturalis Principia Mathematica* translates to *Mathematical Principles of Natural Philosophy.*

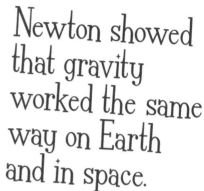

Newton showed that gravity worked the same way on Earth and in space.

Newton's theories led to a better understanding of how our solar system works.

Newton wrote that a force exists between any two objects in the universe. He called the force "gravity." Newton claimed that gravity is stronger between objects of more mass than between objects of less mass. Larger objects create stronger gravity. Smaller objects create weaker gravity. Newton also showed that gravity gets weaker the farther apart the objects are.

Weightlessness Hurts!

Can you imagine being in space and having no weight? Astronauts can drift through their spacecraft as if they were flying. Weightlessness, however, can hurt your body. Space sickness is probably the most common problem. This can include headaches, tiredness, vomiting, and dizziness. Muscles and bones weaken in weightless conditions. Bones lose minerals. Muscles, which don't have to carry the body anymore, lose strength. Astronauts must be very fit before they go into space.

Astronauts use special exercise equipment in space to stay strong.

A Russian astronaut spent 439 days in weightless conditions on a space station.

Engineer and amateur astronomer James Nasmyth built a large 20-inch reflecting telescope that allowed him to chart the moon's surface.

CHAPTER 4

Einstein Explains That Space Bends

Newton showed that all matter attracts all other matter. His laws lasted more than 200 years without change. Many discoveries followed from Newton's laws. Scientists in the 1800s predicted the movement of the planet Uranus. Astronomers noticed, however, that Uranus sometimes moved a bit off course. Using Newton's laws, they guessed that some unknown planet must be near Uranus.

 Larger telescopes allowed for more accurate and detailed observations.

Locating a Mysterious Planet

Scientists predicted where the unknown planet must be. In 1846, a French mathematician named Urbain Le Verrier wrote a letter to an astronomer in Berlin, Germany, to search a specific spot in the sky for the unknown body. The day the letter arrived, a student of the astronomer looked through a powerful telescope and saw the new planet almost exactly where Le Verrier said it would be. Newton's mathematical laws had worked again. The new planet was named Neptune.

Le Verrier explains his discovery to King Louis Philippe of France.

Before becoming known as a physicist, Albert Einstein worked as a clerk in a patent office.

Newton's laws, however, did not always work perfectly. Le Verrier noticed that Mercury, which travels very close to the sun, moved a little differently than the way Newton's laws would predict. It took a young scientist named Albert Einstein to explain this. Einstein revised Newton's laws based on his new idea about space and gravity.

A Groundbreaking Thinker

Albert Einstein was a German-born physicist whose ideas made him one of the world's most influential thinkers of the 20th century. Einstein's theories about time, light, and gravity have changed our view of the world. They have also led to many new inventions.

Timeline of Gravity

1543
Copernicus presents a model of Earth orbiting the sun.

1632
Galileo publishes *Dialogue Concerning the Two Chief World Systems*.

Einstein believed that space bends. He explained that gravity results from the way big objects bend space. But it isn't just big objects that bend space. Einstein said that anything that has mass bends space. Small objects just don't have as much of an effect—as much gravity— as large ones. In other words, your body bends space, just not as much as the sun does!

1686
Isaac Newton publishes his laws of gravity and motion.

1919
Astronomers observe that the sun's gravity bends light.

An Experiment in Space

Imagine you and three friends hold a bedsheet by its corners. Someone places a basketball on the sheet, and it rolls to the middle. The ball sits in the center in a little well it has pushed into the sheet. In Einstein's theory, the ball is like the sun. The sheet is like space.

This illustration shows space, represented by the grid, being bent by the gravity of objects.

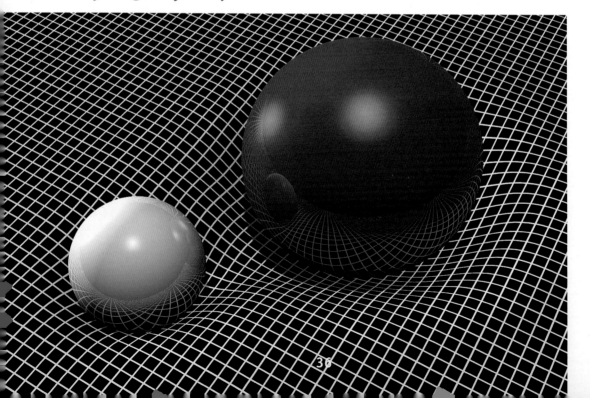

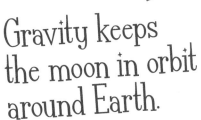

Gravity keeps the moon in orbit around Earth.

Now, let's say someone rolls a tennis ball on the sheet. Rolled gently along an edge of the sheet, the tennis ball will begin to circle the basketball. That is how gravity works, according to Einstein. It bends space so that objects naturally move toward one another. The sun is like the basketball, and the planets are like tennis balls. Big objects, such as the sun, draw smaller objects, such as planets, close to it.

A lighthouse sends a beam of light over the water to show sailors where they will find land.

CHAPTER 5

Gravity, Light, and Stars

Einstein showed us that gravity is a curve in space. Massive objects bend space so other objects move around them. Newton's predictions of planetary movement still worked, but Einstein had improved them. Gravity, however, not only affects things with mass. Einstein theorized that light from a distant star bends when it gets close to the sun.

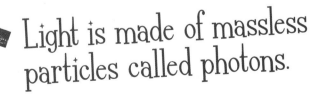

Light is made of massless particles called photons.

Eclipses and Fame

Einstein's theories were published in 1905 and 1916. At first, many scientists doubted him. But in 1919, Arthur Eddington, an English scientist, observed an eclipse of the sun from an island in Africa. He had another team of astronomers observing the eclipse in Brazil. They saw that light from stars in the region around the sun had appeared in a different place during the eclipse. The stars' apparent movement was caused by gravity from the sun bending their light as it passed in front of them. This proved Einstein's theory.

Eddington used photography to prove that the sun's gravity bends light.

Black Holes

Einstein's theory led us to understand black holes. Imagine squeezing a handful of cotton candy into a tiny ball. You would have the same amount of cotton candy, but it takes up less space. It is **dense**. Similarly, when massive stars die, they collapse into much smaller, much denser black holes. Their gravity becomes so strong that light cannot escape.

Astronomers today believe that black holes are located at the center of galaxies.

The planet Venus is visible in the early morning and early evening, even without a telescope.

An astronomer shows a group of school children how to look through a telescope.

An Ever-Changing Science

The story of gravity shows us that science changes. Copernicus changed the way science had thought about the universe for 1,800 years. Then, about 100 years after Copernicus, Newton changed scientific thinking again. It was more than 200 years later when Einstein presented another change to the way we understand gravity. The future is sure to bring more exciting changes in the way we think about our world. ★

Acceleration of falling objects due to Earth's gravity: 32.2 ft./sec.^{2} (9.8 m/sec.^{2})

Weight of a 100-lb. (45.4-kg) person on the moon: 17 lbs. (7.7 kg)

Weight of a 100-lb. (45.4-kg) person on the sun: 2,707 lbs. (1,228 kg)

Speed of light: 186,282 mi./sec. (299,792 km/sec)

Number of objects larger than a softball circling Earth: More than 8,000

Mass of the sun compared to the mass of Earth: 333,000 x Earth

Mass of the moon compared to the mass of Earth: 0.0123 x Earth

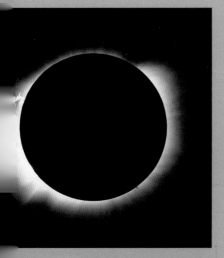

Did you find the truth?

 F Gravity is a magnetic force.

 T Large objects bend space.

Resources

Books

Bailey, Jacqui. *Up, Down, All Around: A Story of Gravity*. Minneapolis: Picture Window Books, 2006.

Boothroyd, Jennifer. *What Holds Us to Earth? A Look at Gravity*. Minneapolis: Lerner Classroom, 2011.

Branley, Franklyn Mansfield. *Gravity Is a Mystery*. New York: Collins, 2007.

Krull, Kathleen. *Albert Einstein*. New York: Viking, 2009.

Krull, Kathleen. *Isaac Newton*. New York: Viking, 2006.

Manolis, Kay. *Gravity*. Minneapolis: Bellwether Media, 2009.

Panchyk, Richard. *Galileo for Kids: His Life and Ideas, 25 Activities*. Chicago: Chicago Review Press, 2005.

Venezia, Mike. *Albert Einstein: Universal Genius*. New York: Children's Press, 2009.

Organizations and Web Sites

A Brief History of Gravity
www-scf.usc.edu/~kallos/gravity.htm
Learn the history of the concept of gravity.

From Apples to Orbits: The Gravity Story
http://library.thinkquest.org/27585
Learn about gravity, its history and effects, and simulate gravitational forces.

Sir Isaac Newton: The Universal Law of Gravitation
http://csep10.phys.utk.edu/astr161/lect/history/newtongrav.html
Read about Newton's laws of motion and gravity.

Places to Visit

American Museum of Natural History
Central Park West at 79th Street
New York, NY 10024
(212) 769-5100
www.amnh.org
See exhibits on Einstein and gravity.

Museo Galileo
Piazza dei Giudici 1
50122 Florence, Italy
+39 055 265 311
www.museogalileo.it/en/index.html
Visit exhibits on Copernicus, Galileo, and the history of science and astronomy.

Important Words

astronomers (uh-STRAH-nuh-mehrz)—scientists who study stars, planets, and space

data (DAY-tuh)—information collected in a place so that something can be done with it

dense (DENS)—crowded or thick

ellipse (i-LIPS)—a flat oval shape

gravity (GRAV-i-tee)—the force that pulls things toward the center of Earth and keeps them from floating away

mass (MAS)—the amount of physical matter that an object contains

matter (MAT-ur)—something that has weight and takes up space, such as a solid, liquid, or gas

molecules (MAH-luh-kyoolz)—the smallest units that a chemical compound can be divided into that still display all of its chemical properties

orbit (OR-bit)—the curved path followed by a moon, planet, or satellite as it circles another planet or the sun

telescopes (TEL-uh-skopez)—instruments that make distant objects seem larger and closer

universe (YOO-nuh-vurs)—all existing matter and space

weight (WATE)—a measurement that shows how heavy someone or something is

Index

Page numbers in **bold** indicate illustrations

Aristotle (philosopher), **12**, 13–14
astronauts, **6**, 7, 28, **29**
astronomers, 16, 17, 18, 19–21, 22, **30**, 31, 32, 35, 40, **42**
atoms, 9
attraction, 8, 25, 31

bending light, 39, **40**
bending space, 35, **36**–37, 39
black holes, **41**
Brahe, Tycho, **17**, 18

Catholic Church, 20, **21**
Copernicus, Nicolaus, 17, 18, 19, **34**, 42

density, 41
Dialogue Concerning the Two Chief World Systems (Galileo Galilei), **20**, **34**

Earth, 8, 10, 11, 14, 15, 16, **24**, 25, 34, 37
eclipses, **40**
Eddington, Arthur, 40
Einstein, Albert, **33**, 34–35, 36, 37, 39, 40, 41, 42
ellipses, 18

falling objects, **8**, 13, 21, 23, **25**, 26

Galilei, Galileo, **19**–**21**, 25, 26, **34**

jump rope games, **11**

Kepler, Johannes, 17–**18**, 26

Le Verrier, Urbain, **32**, 33
light, 35, **38**, 39, **40**, 41
Lyceum school, **12**

marble games, **9**
mass, **9**, 10, 11, 27, 35, 39, 41

mathematics, **14**, 16, 17, 18, 23, **26**, 32
matter, **9**, 10, 31
Mercury, 33
molecules, 9
moon, 8, 15, 19, 23, **24**, 25, 26, **30**, **37**

Nasmyth, James, **30**
Neptune, 32
Newton, Sir Isaac, **22**, 23–24, 26–27, 31, 32, 33, **35**, 39, 42
Newton's laws, **26**, 31, 32, 33, 35, 39

orbit, 8, 15, 16, 18, 19, 24, **27**, 34, **37**

photons, 39
planets, 8, 11, 14, 15, 16, 17, 18, 19, 26, 31, 32, 33, 37, 39, 42
plants, 8
Principia (Sir Isaac Newton), 26
Ptolemy, Claudius, **14**, 15

sizes, **25**, 27, 35, 37
solar system, **27**
space sickness, 28
spacewalking, **6**, 7
sun, 11, 14, 15, 16, 17, 18, 20, 26, 33, 34, 35, 36, 37, 39, 40

telescopes, **19**, **30**, 31, 32, **42**
theories, 25, 26, 27, 34, 36, 39, 40, 41
tides, 24, 26
timeline, **34**–**35**

universe models, 14, **15**, **16**, 17, 18, 20, 34
Uranus, 31

Venus, 19, 42

weight, **9**, **10**, 13, 21
weightlessness, **6**, 7, 28, **29**

About the Author

Matt Mullins holds a master's degree in the history of science from the University of Wisconsin–Madison. Formerly a newspaper reporter, Matt has been a science writer and research consultant for nine years. Matt has written more than two dozen children's books and has written and directed a few short films. He lives in Madison with his son.